A Journey

A Journey with Time

Robert Jaggs-Fowler

Lulu.com
London

To

my mother and father, who laid the foundation stone;

my brother, Richard, who widened the perspective;

and

my wife, Linda,
who lovingly opened the windows in my walls.

Contents

ON THE SUBJECT OF SCHOOL

Foreword

A Journey with Time is an eclectic mix of poems written in the years 2004 to 2008. The title poem was afforded the accolade of 'Highly Commended' in an internet competition in 2006, run by *TooWritePoetry.com* (Northcliffe Publishers). The remainder of the poems have never before been published.

A sense of poetry is in all of us, if only we can be bothered to unlock it. Poetry can be found in everything we experience within our daily lives, if we can just take a few moments to listen to the quiet moments between the hectic ones. I cannot attach any value to my own poetry, apart from the pleasure I have gained from writing it. However, the publication of this, my first collection, is undertaken in the hope that at least some of my poems will strike a chord in one or two readers, and perhaps stimulate a few to try their own hands at writing.

The poems are in no particular order other than that which felt right to me. Amongst them are a variety of conventional styles, as well as attempts at some more contemporary work. I do not claim that they are perfect; many could no doubt be faulted by a more experienced poet. However, in order to assist anyone reading poetry for the first time, I offer a few guidance notes that may be of assistance:

A Poet's Entreaty to Hathor is written in the style of a Shakespearian sonnet. Hathor was the Egyptian goddess of music, love, and beauty.

Japanese styles of poetry are very different from those traditionally found in European cultures. *The Coffin* is in the form of a 'tanka', a non-rhyming format with one stanza (verse) composed of five lines of 5,7,5,7,7 syllables. Another form of Japanese poetry is the 'haiku', again non-rhyming and of one verse. However, a haiku is composed of three lines of 5,7,5 syllables. Haiku usually have reference to nature and seasons, as in the *Haiku from the Galapagos Islands* and *July in England*. The attachment of a title to these poems is a deviation from tradition, as haiku are normally left to speak for themselves

Communing with History is in a form known as a villanelle. Villanelles are somewhat complicated, with five stanzas of three lines, plus one final stanza of four lines. The 1st line of the initial stanza is repeated as the last line of the 2nd and 4th stanzas; the 3rd line of the 1st stanza is repeated as the last line for the 3rd and 5th stanzas. These two motif lines then become the penultimate and final lines of the poem. The rhyme scheme is *aba,* i.e. the 1st line of each verse rhymes with the 3rd line of the same verse.

Life's Refrain is a Chaucerian roundel: three stanzas of 3, 3 and 4 lines, with the 1st line of the 1st verse being repeated as the 3rd line of the 2nd verse, and finally as the 4th line of the 3rd verse.

Most people are familiar with limericks and will hopefully appreciate that they are supposed to be light hearted; often bordering on the ribald. It is additionally hoped that their inclusion in this book, under the collective heading *On the Subject of School*, will not be the cause of offence to anyone.

I have often been asked how I decide on the subject for a poem. The truth is that I find it hard to write to order. Some of my personal favourites have come about spontaneously, often at moments of intense

[11]

emotion, and therefore have stories behind them. One such poem is *An Elegy to a Swallow,* which resulted from my necessity to shelter in a church porch from a storm raging on the rather isolated island of Lundy in the Bristol Channel. The beautiful, but dead, swallow lying just within the entrance of the porch jarred with the stone building and the force of the storm, and hence a poem was born. There are clues for the origins of many others, either within the titles or within the poems themselves. However, I feel that poetry is best left to speak to the reader, and for the reader thereby to find his or her own special meaning. I will therefore say nothing more on this subject.

I have often been accused by my brother of 'not living in the real world'. My long-suffering and very tolerant wife is also used to my frequent periods of deep introversion. There can be little doubt that the writing of poetry is a rather solitary pursuit, and perhaps a degree of worldly detachment is required to capture the gist of those 'quiet moments' in life when the inner voice is struggling to be heard. If that is the case, then perhaps this slim volume will be of some consolation to my family and make them feel that their frustrations and sufferings have not been in vain. Regardless, I am certainly grateful for my wife's long-standing, forbearance, particularly in bearing the brunt of my ramblings and my enthusiastic first-readings.

I take full responsibility for the content of the poems, and for any mistakes contained within this book. All the poems are my own work and, with the exception of some attributed sources, I have not consciously used work from elsewhere.

Finally, I am more than happy to enter into correspondence with anyone who might wish to comment on any of the poems and, in this respect, I can be contacted at: r.jaggs-fowler@theretreat-barton.com.

Thank you for joining me in *A Journey with Time*. I hope it brings you pleasure.

ROBERT M. JAGGS-FOWLER
Barton upon Humber
August 2008

[14]

A Poet's Entreaty to Hathor

If music knows the route to where man's soul
resides within, then let its soothing balm
ignite that unseen force which makes me whole.
Sweet melody, I pray, commence your charm.
Let the swinging rhythm of jazz and blues
regenerate that spark of life once more
with its syncopated beat. Hear me my muse:
guide from my pen those words she may adore.
As I sit here, surrounded by my books,
fuelling a melancholic mind with gin,
to you my lost imagination looks.
Free the prose that my lover's heart will win!
Melodic arrows, cause our lives to meet.
Through you, with her, my life becomes complete.

Melancholia

An elusive emotion of countless forms;
being a dark winter's evening; candle light;
an old armchair next to a log-fire;
a Labrador lying at one's feet.

It hides in the finest of peaty, malt whisky,
or as a row of leather-bound, antiquarian books.
It may be a rain-lashed island cottage,
or run with the wind around a ramshackle old house.

For hours, it sits clad in an old dressing gown,
with a mahogany pipe of aromatic tobacco,
or, accompanied by the aroma of freshly ground coffee,
be discovered in a slice of cheese on toast.

Some days it lies silently as frost on a hillside,
sits under the yew in a country church yard,
chooses to turn into a well-tendered garden,
or the meditative cloister in a monastic retreat.

At times, such as on a warm summer's evening,
it whiles away hours playing tenor sax,
or, when a particular mood takes it,
can be heard in a nightclub, singing the blues.

Being an adaptable concept, over the centuries
it has taken on guises, perpetuated its lot:
such as Mahler's 5th Symphony, Turner's landscapes,
or the pondering poetry of W. B. Yeats.

But, despite all of its many disguises,
it surely remains misunderstood, save by
a few who'd recognise its store of energy
and welcome it home as oft as they could.

Beside the Brook

Suppose that,
besides this babbling brook,
we were to live out our days,
content with knowing
that time had stood still, simply
to let this moment
live,
forever.

Suppose that
the very waters here before us,
which tumble onwards to
their journey's end,
were to cease their flow, simply
to reflect our image
for
evermore.

Suppose that
the clouds within this
blue, afternoon sky
should suspend their flight and
allow the sun to bathe this spot
where we now sit, in
warmth,
unceasing.

Suppose that
the very air we breathe
should in a moment
still itself such that
our whispered words simply
hung in the air to form a
constant
echo.

Then, I would not yearn
after the life forgone;
but I would take your hand
and smile at your sunlit face,
and whisper softly those words
destined to linger on
when this day is finally no more:
'I love you'.

The Coffin

A lifetime encased:
your boundless intellect and
energy, swathed in
a vast cloak of achievement,
simply borne by two trestles.

An Elegy to a Swallow

Fallen acrobat of the skies:
your mastery of the air
dissolved in one
false turn,
leaving this frail,
broken body
lying in a
cold, stone porch
of a church on a
windswept isle, far from
your native Africa.

Your form's beauty
jars with these harsh
surroundings.
Such
perfection
deserves a more
fitting end
to a life of
hope.

continued

[21]

I see in your
discordant loss the
reflection
of that hidden
by life's magnificence:
the final,
cruel truth
that all splendour is
ultimately
lost,

and I mourn
for my
fallen acrobat of the skies.

Climbing Ingleborough on Good Friday

Parked in a lay-by in Chapel-le-Dale,
boots tightly laced,
and with a laden pack,
we passed through a latched gate onto the fell,
marching the route we've come to know so well.

Across grassy pastures with lambs a-new,
past limestone kilns
and fresh trickling streams,
greeting passers-by as though us they knew:
no down-turned eyes, as city dwellers do.

Over trodden paths and a cinder track,
then limestone slabs
placed through boggy peat -
thick seams of history laid down in black:
ancient tales of tree-scapes the hills now lack.

Far away from the holiday masses -
the traffic queues
and car parks quite full,
we're where the grouse midst the heather dashes,
and wind, our senses splendidly bashes.

continued

Under high white clouds and a sun-filled sky,
past Braithwaite Wife Hole
and through Humphrey Bottom,
we climb rock-strewn slopes where the curlews fly;
above us the plateau - our goal is nigh.

Reaching the summit means ample reward:
sandwiches and tea
in the lee of a cairn;
about us a panorama quite broad;
Pennines resplendent: the work of our Lord?

Around us a skyline of rolling tops:
there's Pen-y-ghent,
with Whernside yonder;
the Ribblesdale viaduct 'tween hills, hops.
Nowhere in sight is the spectre of shops!

Hang-gliders beneath coloured canopies,
float by on thermals,
as we descend
with sun-reddened faces and aching knees.
Life is good: freedom and health are the keys.

Morning on Lough Eske, Donegal

Mist enveloped hills:
a collective shroud of the voices,
long lost to a troubled,
Irish past.

An evocation of distant memories.

For centuries, such vapours have steered
countless pens of rising emerald stars
into the literary firmament;
their words percolating the heady mix of
peat-smoked rooms, viewed through
deep draughts of snow-capped raven-black,
or the fiery fumes of malted amber.

Khayyam's long-risen hunter forms
a pale ghost beyond the
dull, dank, dripping sentinels
on the lough's unseen shore,
boughs swaying with the haunting,
faded strains of last evening's
beaten bodrán and frenzied fiddle.

Omnipresent echoes of unrequited expectation.

Between Chapters

*"...six ruffians seen through an open window playing cards at night
at a small French railway junction where there was a water-
mill..."*

T. S. Eliot

Dishonour, vice, greed, hate, fraud, distrust:
I will not join your loathsome band,
for you are the embodiment of my inadequacies;
the substance of my basest nightmares.
My darkness is preferable to the false warmth
and sleights of hand of your dissonant sextet.

I do not fear you now.
This junction on life's journey is but a
transient halt in foreign territory.
With dawn, the points will change; a fresh track
will lead from your abhorrent falsehoods.
The wheel of my life's work will turn once more.

The Ballad of the Reverend Heaven

Reverend Hudson Grosset Heaven
once lived on the Island of Lundy
(lying just off the west coast of Devon)
with no place to work on a Sunday.

His family sold, to the mainland,
granite from Lundy's quarry,
and thus their life on the island
was devoid of financial worry.

After the death of William, his father,
in eighteen eighty-three,
Hudson got himself in a lather,
over a vision only he could see.

A church was all that he wished for,
'To the Glory of God,' he said.
'Somewhere to preach the Holy Law
and for the islanders to wed.'

The late Mrs Langworthy's legacy,
(in the best of our English tradition -
it absolved the donor from heresy),
helped achieve his lifetime's ambition.

continued

[27]

From yonder Ilfracombe came a mason
who, hewn granite, skilfully weighed,
and, from the start setting to with a pace on,
in no time had the foundations laid.

In 1896, it was completed,
for just under five thousand pounds.
Two hundred there could be seated,
called by tintinnabulous sounds.

So, Reverend Hudson Grosset Heaven
had his church, in gothic style;
though few knew of its secret, quite pagan,
which is best seen from a seat in the aisle.

For, on the day of the Summer Solstice,
from the west, watching the setting sun falter,
with a precision which, to the builder does justice,
the light illuminates the cross on the altar.

That completes my story from Lundy,
an island off the west coast of Devon,
which, through the work of Hudson's each Sunday,
became known as the Kingdom of Heaven.

The Keys

The annual ritual.
Office closed early, cheap wine, paper plates,
sausage rolls, mince pies, false *bonhomie*.
It's subtle: like watching an old-
fashioned movie; no words spoken. Two
actors, a silent witness and the keys.
Never have keys been more fascinating.
He is the last to arrive, the first to go.
Keys on table, alcohol declined - a
long drive home to the country awaited.
A secretary toys distractedly
with the fob, arranges the keys into
a fan and separates one bronze Yale key
from the rest. Avoiding eye contact, he
sets a Chubb key next to the Yale and leaves.
Some time later, she picks up the keys and
exits. That is it; the message received.
No one notices but me; but I'd played
last year. Out with the old...

Communing with History

Relaxed within the country I adore,
in solace brought by peaceful solitude,
I feel the hint of shadows gone before.

If nature's storms may, through the valleys, roar,
lithe music of the wind, come play to me -
relaxed within the country I adore.

Open my heart and let my spirit soar,
as, freed from binding chains of daily toil,
I feel the hint of shadows gone before.

Though seeing ghosts of old leaves some in awe,
I am in tune with those fragmented souls,
relaxed within the country I adore.

It matters not if I am rich or poor:
in quiet moments when my soul's at ease,
I feel the hint of shadows gone before.

Astride the hills, on cliffs or valley floor,
when tumbling mists of time pervade the land,
relaxed within the country I adore,
I feel the hint of shadows gone before.

Choleric Musings
(On the day Gordon Brown became Prime Minister)

'I have heard the need for change.
...now let the work of change begin.'

Footage of journeys along The Mall;
political metamorphosis by Royal Assent.
Traditional photo-shoot at number 10
of this nation's primary (Scottish) gent.

'I remember words...which matter a great deal today:
"I will try my utmost".'

Forgive a somewhat jaded view
from a veteran of decades past.
Successive governments have promised as much:
will your offerings be the ones to last?

'I will build a government that uses all the talents.'

Are you capable of bringing stability?
Will your changes be climacteric?
Will patients see improvements they seek?
Are your sound-bites empty rhetoric?

Postcard from Peru

High above the Colca Mountain ranges,
beneath the cloudless, blue, Andean skies,
in a land little transformed by changes,
the sacred condor flies.

Beneath the snow-capped mountains hid by haze,
observed by villagers in clothes quite gay,
llamas, vicunas and alpacas graze
and haunting pan-pipes play.

O'er the waters of Lake Titicaca,
on floating islands of totora reed,
the Uros people chew leaves of coca,
and fish to herons feed.

Braving earth tremors in Arequipa,
well-sustained by Pisco Sours,
English tourists haggle to buy cheaper:
the dollar here empowers.

Via the catacombs of San Francisco,
a shaman of the Island of the Sun,
through cactus-strewn plains of the Altiplano,
travellers' days are done.

Behold the Ice Maiden, Juanita;
the Garden of Lovers in Lima Bay;
the Orient Express is a feature:
rolling on – no delay.

The towering walls of Machu Picchu
instil with awe, inspire, expand the mind.
Support the local trade, we beseech you:
'Just one sol – that's most kind!'

From the ancient tombs of Sillustani,
down the pre-Inca terraced, rocky slopes,
to borders protected by the army,
Peru portrays its hopes.

The Emotive Cornucopia

(After *The Doctor* by Sir Luke Fildes, Oil on canvas, 1891 – Tate
Gallery)

The sick child's home speaks of poverty:
bare walls, wooden beams, stone floors,
rough-hewn furniture.
A solitary lamp illuminates her bed –
two mismatched chairs;
coats as coverings.

The sick child's home speaks of despair.
In the shadows, her distraught mother
and dignified, powerless father,
his energy focused through the doctor.
A helpless triumvirate
in the face of the anonymous.

The sick child's home speaks of compassion.
Antibiotics unknown, the doctor,
the embodiment of their hope and trust,
ponders her fate;
a tonic bottle, feeding cup and water jug
his only armoury against the nameless.

Yet,
despite the depths of emotions,
simplistic surroundings
and human frailty,
there resides unfathomable wealth:

amidst all else,

the sick child's home speaks of love.

Haiku from the Galapagos Islands

Marine iguanas
trail home through volcanic ash.
Galapagos dusk.

***

One century old,
a tortoise views our approach:
footsteps of Darwin.

A Journey with Time

I remember not the moment when Time,
That unseen force,
Rescued me from obscurity,
Plucking me aboard as though I were
A mailbag taken from the station gibbet;
And, having bade me ride it for a while,
Time moved on.

Relentless was the journey there began,
From a place unknown,
The destination unshared,
Without pause for thought,
No halts to savour the moment,
Opportunities snatched whilst one may,
As Time ran on.

Like an unbroken thread
Linking me to those who
Had journeyed so long ago,
Stretching out towards those yet to board,
Slotting places and events, through which we passed,
Into Life's continuum without a pause,
Time weaved on.

continued

Pathos, Drama, Passion, Melancholy and Mirth
Travelled with me as the years went past,
Each lending me a little of their worth as
Some scenes flowed serenely by, whilst
Others called for me to play my part, as though
I was an actor on Shakespeare's worldly stage;
And Time played on.

I feasted heartily at Life's festive board,
Drank merrily from its wondrous store,
Seized each day, not knowing when
The last grains of sand would fall and
The hand of Death would on my shoulder lay,
Bidding me to make my journey's end as, without me,
Time passed on.

A Litany for Life

A blessing on the month of January,
the Water Bearer's realm.

A blessing on my land of birth,
steadfast with English roots.

A blessing on grammar school education,
a passport through society.

A blessing on my beautiful wife,
the bearer of life's sun.

A blessing on the Yorkshire Dales
wherein resides my soul.

A blessing on syncopated rhythm
reflecting the riffs of life.

A blessing on my walking boots,
the printing press and vintage wine.

A blessing on experiences past,
and those destined to come.

A blessing on whosoever ordained
this blessed life of mine.

An Ode to Literary Tomes

Sentient keepers of the written word,
what secrets lie within your treasured boards!
So many voices waiting to be heard
above the lure of electronic bauds.
I cannot tell a lie: I am beguiled
by leather spines embossed with gilded leaves,
which sit alluringly on wooden shelves,
barred zealously from friends who would be thieves.
Though on the desk and floor you may be piled,
your charms transcend and must not be defiled;
for books are friends if one takes time and delves.

Life's Refrain

The church bells rang for you today.
As water poured upon your head,
'I name this child,' the vicar said.

Betrothed, then vows without delay.
To tell the world that you have wed,
the church bell rang for you today.

'For this departed soul we pray.'
The priest, in solemn homage, led
the mourners, who prayed for the dead.
The church bells rang for you today.

Be Cautious Ye People of the Isle of Man

Misted isle within the Irish Sea,
whose ancestors caused the Spanish to flee,
who greeted Celt and Viking to your shores
and whose ancient parliament still proclaims your laws,
stand proud amidst the British Isles;
resist the call of Brussels, as it beguiles
you to relinquish your tax haven;
remember the call of Odin's Raven.

Scattered through many a remote location
are the symbols that age this maritime nation:
Celtic and Viking stone memorial crosses,
erected by your forebears to honour their losses.
Then behold the great towers of Castle Rushen,
home of the last Norse King of Mann, whose men
gave life and limb to defend your land.
Reduce not their mighty rocks to sand.

See Rushen Abbey: ancient seat of Manx Christianity,
and Peel Castle: peopled by brothers of divinity.
Cast not aside the miners of Laxey, whose wheel
kept mines dry as they toiled for a meagre meal.
Neither forget the pioneering spirit of teachers
of the Old Grammar School, speaking out to beseech us
that the right of all children, regardless of station,
was to at least be given a sound education.

The poetic Manx dialect of T. E. Brown, unleashed,
with rhyming stanzas, memorials to lives at Cregneash.
And, whilst not wishing back the Old House of Keys,
bring not your three-legged symbol down on its knees.
Be proud of the millenary ceremonies of Tynwald Hill,
and let future generations there proclaim that, still,
in keeping with the spirit of the god, Manannan,
free of interference from Europe stands the Isle of Man.

ON THE SUBJECT OF SCHOOL

Puppy Love

There was once a sixth former called Meacher,
who fell madly in love with his teacher.
Against all fervent hope,
she declined to elope.
But he did all he could to beseech her.

Selective Uptake

Science, English Lit. and History
remained constant mysteries to me.
But, all sex education
I pursued with elation,
as the practical lessons were free.

A Reformed Character

It is said that the Head of St. Bede
caught a boy midst a devilish deed.
When told not to smoke,
nor to snort coke,
he conformed, and now only takes speed.

Corporal Punishment

The Head of St. Trinian's once said,
'The one thing I positively dread
is, when given the cane,
the girls love the pain,
so I issue detentions instead.'

Forbidden Fruit

It was against the squash court wall,
between the gym and our school pool,
when I kissed Mary
where she was hairy,
and it wasn't her lips, I recall.

Liberating Lesson

'It is a wonderful thing, education,'
said the boy in a state of elation,
as he outlined the feature
adorning the teacher,
'Thank goodness for emancipation.'

Careers Advice

You must, when in class, pay attention to me.
Education's important; you'll need a degree.
With post-nominal letters,
you'll not envy your betters:
Primus inter pares you'll be.

English Report

'Young man, you'll never a writer be,
with these stories as presented to me.
You've not edited a word
and your grammar's absurd;
do not begin to attempt poetry!'

Life's Denouement
(After Old Man by Elizabeth Jennings)

Do not be fooled by my inaction.
My silent world is not what it seems.
You see an old man confined by
a bed, a chair, a room.
You perceive tranquillity, yet
I have no need for communication.

Chairbound?

I am not even earthbound.

I have earned my freedom from
materialistic chains.
Knowledge now powers my
unencumbered travel. I exist
disassociated from your reality.

You think you tend to an old man.
Yet, you are satellite images
to where my world revolves.
That shadow is the real me:
waking with dawn, slipping away
by midday and, for now, returning
with the setting sun.

Time knows no boundaries.
Age is not what it seems;
death, a powerful invocation.
Your delusion is
my ultimate illusion.

I am not the old man you see before you.

I am.

The Library

I am your favourite;
the first you enter each morning,
the last you leave at night.
You wear my four walls like a shell:
your escape from reality.
Through me, you can be
anyone,
anywhere,
anytime.
I am the
externalisation of what your brain
can never be.
Although you conceived me,
nurtured me over many years,
I am something you can
only aspire to.
I am overflowing; I suffer from a
literary obesity, yet
you continue to feed me.
You admire me for
my beauty, my age, my venerability,
and envy me
for my knowledge.

I now speak with a
thousand accumulated voices, but
you only have time to
converse with a few.
Yet, we are symbiotic:
without me, you would be bereft;
without you, I would cease to exist.
Though my appetite is insatiable, so
is your desire to see me advance. For
I represent
your past,
your present,
your future,
as well as those aspirations you
will never achieve.
I am your obsession,
your saviour and
your nemesis.
In me, you have created
your likeness
as well as
your antithesis.

A Ballad in Memory of the Irish Famine 1845-1850

Outside the town of Donegal
lies a burial site to see;
such poignancy between four walls
is a lesson for the hunger-free.

> *The potato crop is black with blight,*
> *and we've not a joint to carve,*
> *yet fear not, for the English will see us right;*
> *they will not see us starve.*

One hundred and fifty years have passed
waving famine a long goodbye,
yet many questions still get asked
of those remains here piled on high.

> *The potato crop is black with blight,*
> *and we've not a joint to carve,*
> *yet fear not, for the English will see us right;*
> *they will not see us starve.*

Who dared oppose, when Peel did try
to import corn, or change the laws?
why did two million people die,
or chance their lives on distant shores?

The potato crop is black with blight,
and we've not a joint to carve,
yet fear not, for the English will see us right;
they will not see us starve.

Economists cried *'laissez-faire'*,
whilst landlords demanded their rents,
and to the courts, took those who dared
poach fish, and thus, transported, went.

The potato crop is black with blight,
and we've not a joint to carve,
yet fear not, for the English will see us right;
they will not see us starve.

At Peel's behest, a group was formed,
known as the Relief Commission;
and, seeking aid, the people swarmed,
reliant on fair decisions.

The potato crop is black with blight,
and we've not a joint to carve,
yet fear not, for the English will see us right;
they will not see us starve.

But those whose need, God knows, was most,
were quite unfit for building roads.
For them, the Workhouse was their host,
if space be found in such abodes.

[53]

The potato crop is black with blight,
and we've not a joint to carve,
yet fear not, for the English will see us right:
they will not see us starve.

English charities sent their aid;
and the Quakers built large soup pots,
but still, young dying children laid
amidst the dead just left to rot.

The potato crop is black with blight,
and we've not a joint to carve,
yet fear not, for the English will see us right:
they will not see us starve.

A widow and her children plead
as, evicted from their hovel
at the whim of a landlord's greed,
they have no choice but to grovel.

The potato crop is black with blight,
and we've not a joint to carve,
yet fear not, for the English will see us right:
they will not see us starve.

From typhus fever they must flee,
for the doctors are dying too.
But food is on its way – you'll see;
The Act of Union will come through.

[54]

The potato crop is black with blight,
and we've not a joint to carve,
yet fear not, for the English will see us right:
they will not see us starve.

Yet, for all the talk, five years passed
and a solution was not found.
Thus, to distant shores, Ireland cast,
to start new lives in fertile ground.

So, if the potato crop is black with blight,
and you've not a joint to carve,
best look West, for the English ne'er saw us right:
their politicians watched us starve.

The Pearl Choker

Early morning.
You lie discarded on the dressing table,
resting from the night before.
A surprise gift, I recollect how
I once pretended to
strangle your mistress,
mentally marking where my fingers touched and
carrying the size to the jewellers the following day.
Fastening your clasp, her hair
falls over my fingers and,
as I stroke the three strands of pearls,
I imagine
the tracery of her fine neck over which
you lay.
I caress the central ruby,
remembering the delicate notch
between her collar bones, which I
outline in the air with my finger.
You still carry the fragrance of
her perfume, causing
my back to ripple.
I am looking into the
Champagne sparkle of her eyes;
I kiss her lips and
once more, we are
dancing, dancing, dancing…

There's no one here at the moment

Where is the spark of life that's called man's soul -
the driving force which was the man I knew;
that power once underwriting every goal?

I cannot recognise you lying here,
surrounded by tubes and bottles and screens.
'Fight back!' I plead, and wipe a way a tear.

An Incantation on the Subject of Time

For I will consider Time,
> as it underwrites my life.

For I will consider having being born two weeks late:
> I am yet to catch up.

For I will consider Time wasted:
> that which is lost cannot be re-gained.

For I will consider the young,
> as they know not what they squander.

For I will consider those who profess boredom
> and will requisition their surplus time.

For I will consider ageing;
> time passes faster for the old.

For I will consider the twenty-four hour day;
> I wish it could be thirty-six.

For I will consider deadlines,
> as they dominate my working day.

For I will consider sleep
> and how it might be creatively harnessed.

For I will consider Henry Longfellow
> and his great men 'toiling upward in the night'.

For I will consider eternity:
> what magnitudes could be achieved?

For I will consider Rudyard Kipling
> and his 'sixty seconds worth of distance run'.

For I will consider Time as life's currency,
      by which measure I am a pauper.
For I will consider founding a Time Bank
      and will grant myself a large overdraft.
For I will consider such great ambitions,
      as I have no time to bring them to fruition.

July in England

Unseasonal rains.
Bouquet of chilled chardonnay:
summer in a glass.

A Writer's Prayer

Lord,
may the cloud of words,
which is omnipresent over my head,
with your blessing, pour down
as a shower upon me.
Let it percolate through my brain and,
via the conduit of this pen,
reappear as sentences,
formed and erudite,
upon the paper in front of me.
May those sentences be the source of pleasure to many,
provoke thought in at least a few,
and be the cause of harm to no one.

Amen

Finis